Delivery DRONES

Joe Ferry

ReferencePoint
Press

San Diego, CA

About the Author

Joe Ferry is a retired reporter and editor who has written fifteen nonfiction books for the middle school market. He lives in Montgomery County, Pennsylvania.

For more information, contact:
ReferencePoint Press, Inc.
PO Box 27779
San Diego, CA 92198
www.ReferencePointPress.com

LIBRARY OF CONGRESS CATALOGING-IN-PUBLICATION DATA

Names: Ferry, Joe, author.
Title: Delivery drones / by Joe Ferry.
Description: San Diego, CA : ReferencePoint Press, [2021] | Series: World of drones | Includes bibliographical references and index.
Identifiers: LCCN 2020002097 (print) | LCCN 2020002098 (ebook) | ISBN 9781682828298 (library binding) | ISBN 9781682828304 (ebook)
Subjects: LCSH: Aeronautics, Commercial--Freight--Juvenile literature. | Drone aircraft--Juvenile literature. | Delivery of goods--Juvenile literature.
Classification: LCC HE9788 .F47 2021 (print) | LCC HE9788 (ebook) | DDC 387.7/44--dc23
LC record available at https://lccn.loc.gov/2020002097
LC ebook record available at https://lccn.loc.gov/2020002098

CONTENTS

A Revolution in Delivery Service

In November 2016 a New Zealand couple became the first people in the world to have pizza delivered to them by an unmanned aerial vehicle, otherwise known as a drone. Actually, it was two pizzas—a Peri-Peri Chicken and a Chicken and Cranberry—that Domino's flew to the backyard of Emma and Johnny Norman's home in Whangaparaoa, about 20 miles (32 km) north of Auckland. The entire flight took about five minutes and came just three months after Domino's announced a partnership with Flirtey, an independent drone delivery service.

By all accounts, the Normans enjoyed their piping-hot pizzas even more than if they had been brought to the couple's front door by a regular delivery person. "The delivery was a lot quicker and it was most certainly fresher and hotter. We are really excited to see how this proceeds,"[1] they said.

To many people, the thought of pilotless vehicles whizzing overhead delivering everything from clothes to groceries to skateboards seems like something out of a science fiction novel. But some of the world's biggest e-commerce companies are in a fierce race for early control of the drone delivery market, especially in the United States. They are spending hundreds of millions of dollars to design and develop drone delivery systems that are cost effective, energy efficient, environmentally friendly, unobtrusive, and most of all, safe to operate.

Meeting Customer Demand

The pizza-by-drone demonstration in New Zealand was little more than a publicity stunt at the time. Even so, it provided tangible evidence that drone deliveries are not only possible but are also a probable solution as companies struggle for new ways to keep up with customer demands for faster shipping times. Since the Normans received their pizza, several companies have been busy designing, developing, and testing drone delivery programs. They hope to one day soon convince the Federal Aviation Administration (FAA) that they can operate safely. The FAA is the government agency that regulates air traffic in the United States. Before businesses can deliver their goods by drone, they will need to convince the FAA to relax its rules and allow widespread commercial programs. A few companies, including Google and UPS, have been successful in getting FAA approval to operate limited drone delivery programs to consumers in parts of North Carolina and Virginia.

unobtrusive

Not blatant, arresting, or aggressive; not easily observed or noticed

In addition to Google and UPS, e-commerce powerhouses Amazon and Walmart are among the biggest companies competing to see who can be the fastest to put a delivery drone program in place in the United States. Other companies, such as Uber, are also looking to get in on the action. Even the US Postal Service (USPS) is investigating ways it can deliver some packages by drones. Plus, there are independent drone delivery services, such as Flirtey, based in Australia, and Zipline International, headquartered in the United States. These companies are developing partnerships to deliver everything from blood in Africa to vaccines on islands in the South Pacific to school supplies in Indonesia.

As of 2020 the United States lagged behind the rest of the world in developing successful drone delivery services (mostly because of strict government regulations). China, for example,

In a scene that would previously have been described as science fiction, a drone with a package secured to its underside heads for its destination. Drone delivery is already a reality in some places.

was actively using drones to transport goods to people living in remote villages. Companies in Switzerland, Finland, Iceland, China, Australia, and Singapore were in various stages of developing commercial drone delivery operations. A second wave of countries—Germany, Dubai, and Canada—was not far behind.

Last-Mile Delivery

Drones are a natural evolution in the way products are delivered. From steamships to railroads, from the Pony Express to modern delivery services such as FedEx and UPS, advances in how goods move from place to place have helped reshape the world. But there is still room for improvement, and that is where drones can make a difference. Current methods of transportation are not always fast enough, especially when it comes to delivering medical supplies or other necessities in hard-to-reach areas. The transportation of goods has also added to the increase of CO_2

gas emitted into the atmosphere. In the United States alone, according to some estimates, 27 percent of greenhouse gas emissions come from transportation. With their emission-less, battery-powered engines, drones could make a significant difference by taking thousands of vehicles off the streets.

Delivery by drone is also appealing because it can solve the unpredictable and most expensive final leg of the journey, known in the package and food delivery business as the last mile. The *last mile* refers to the final link in the delivery chain—a chain that begins with the grower or manufacturer and ends with a product being delivered to the customer's doorstep. Companies have pretty much figured out the most efficient ways to get products from growers and manufacturers to their fulfillment warehouses with a vast network of planes, trains, ships, and trucks. These modes of transport work reasonably well; the high volume of products to be delivered keeps the cost per piece relatively small.

But the process of getting the product from the warehouse to the customer's doorstep can be complicated and expensive because it is dependent on weather conditions, traffic flow, and the work ethic of human employees. By some estimates, that so-called last mile can account for about 53 percent of the total cost of delivering an item to the customer. So, for a customer who pays $10 for shipping, more than half of that amount is the cost of someone just dropping off the package on the customer's doorstep. Amazon, for example, made more than 5 billion deliveries to its Prime customers in 2017 at a cost of about $200 billion, an average of about $4 each. The overwhelming majority of those packages were small enough to be handled by a drone, which many experts believe can make that last mile a smooth, cost-effective delivery option. Some estimates suggest that each delivery made by drone could cost as little as $1. Whichever company comes up with the answer first will have an incredible impact on the way customers shop for generations to come.

Obstacles to Overcome

Before drone delivery becomes a common part of everyday life, however, there are many logistical obstacles that must be overcome. The regulatory hurdles are high. Testing is expensive and time consuming. Priorities include the safety of people on the ground and the security of packages as they fly through the air. Companies must find foolproof ways to avoid mid-air collisions with other aircraft, birds, and buildings and to cope with quickly changing weather conditions—and even the possibility of a drone carrying valuable cargo being electronically hijacked and diverted to another location. Then they must figure out the best way to physically place the package at the customer's doorstep. Some proposals include parachutes. Others envision packages being lowered to the ground by tether while the drone hovers 50 feet (15.2 m) above the ground. Even something as seemingly simple as how the package is released when it arrives at its destination is the subject of intensive research.

logistical

Related to the planning, implementation, and coordination of the details of a business or other operation

Substantial progress has been made on all these fronts, yet skeptics doubt that widespread drone delivery of consumer goods will ever become reality, especially in densely populated urban areas. In addition to logistical challenges, critics say that consumers will never put up with drones in their neighborhoods at all hours of the day and night. In England, for example, where Amazon was conducting tests, some residents were reported to have been "absolutely horrified"[2] about noise and potential damage to historic sites. Before drones gain widespread acceptance, companies will have to convince the public that the convenience of ultra-quick delivery outweighs any effects on quality of life. "Drones and urban delivery robots have a lot of issues to overcome,"[3] says industry analyst Bart De Muynck.

Despite the significant challenges, companies continue to invest hundreds of millions of dollars in research and development in hopes of someday making commercial delivery drones a common sight in cities and towns around the world. The FAA predicted that sales of drones for a wide range of commercial purposes would grow from 600,000 in 2016 to 2.7 million in 2020. Amazon characterizes the likelihood of drone deliveries this way: "It looks like science fiction, but it's real. One day, seeing Prime Air vehicles will be as normal as seeing mail trucks on the road."[4] While that day is not here yet, it very well could be in the near future.

CHAPTER 1

The Race to Be First in the United States

On a sunny Friday afternoon in October 2019, Susie and Paul Sensmeier played a small but important role in making American history. The retirees, who live in Christiansburg, Virginia, watched intently as a small drone zipped toward their house. Operated by Wing, an offshoot of Google's parent company, Alphabet, the aircraft approached with a high-pitched whine, then hovered in the clear blue sky above their front lawn for a few moments. It gently lowered a FedEx box containing a new vest for Susie, a birthday present from her husband.

Across the street, several people, including officials from the White House and the FAA, looked on with interest. They were there to witness the first-ever commercial delivery by a drone in the United States. While drones previously had delivered medical samples to hospitals, prescriptions to patients, and food items to customers during limited testing programs in some parts of the country, the delivery to the Sensmeier's house was a milestone for the drone delivery industry. This was no test. Nor was it a publicity stunt. A real product was delivered from a real company to a real customer. "I love new things," Susie, age eighty-one, told a reporter after the drone had departed. "New technology. A new vest. New experiences. You don't get a lot of those at my age."[5]

Beginning of a Revolution?

The Sensmeiers' experience might be the beginning of a dramatic shift in the way e-commerce deliveries happen. Consumers have increasingly demanded faster delivery times for their purchases. At first, two-day shipping was the innovation, then one-day shipping, then same-day shipping. Now drones offer the promise of one-hour delivery—or even faster.

But it could be years before Google's Wing or another company is able to establish regular consumer delivery programs around the United States. Satisfying government regulators, overcoming logistical obstacles, and gaining public acceptance will take time. Still, with billions of dollars in revenue at stake, several companies are competing to see who will be the first to launch a full-scale consumer drone delivery service.

Getting to the point at which Susie Sensmeier could receive her birthday vest by delivery drone took much longer than a lot of people expected. Among them was Jeff Bezos, chief executive officer (CEO) of Amazon, who made a startling prediction in December 2013. Speaking on a television show about the Christmas season shopping, Bezos announced that his company was working on a plan to deliver small packages to residential customers in less than thirty minutes. His proposal called for a fleet of unmanned aerial vehicles, or drones. The drones would sit on the end of conveyor belts in hundreds of fulfillment centers around the country, waiting to pick up a package and deliver it anywhere within 10 miles (16.1 km) in under half an hour.

At the time, many people thought Bezos was joking or that he was just creating some valuable hype for his company during the busy holiday season. Skeptics scoffed at Amazon's video showing a drone delivering a package to a suburban doorstep. It looked like something from a futuristic cartoon, they said. But Bezos was serious about the future of delivery drones. "It will work, and it will happen, and it's going to be a lot of fun,"[6] he insisted at the time.

Since Bezos made his prediction, three other major e-commerce companies—Google, UPS, and Walmart—have

Amazon CEO Jeff Bezos predicted as early as 2013 that drones would someday be used to deliver packages to residential customers.

joined in the competition to be the first to offer a viable drone delivery program to their US customers. Each has embarked on its own research, development, and testing. The USPS is also looking at making some deliveries by drone, especially in rural areas where the distance between stops makes traditional mail delivery inefficient.

As 2019 came to a close, however, only two companies had established anything close to resembling a drone delivery program for consumers: Google Wing and UPS Flight Forward. Wing's service was limited to a small town in Virginia. At the same time, Flight Forward was operating a drone delivery program at WakeMed Health in North Carolina, delivering blood and other medical specimens between facilities within the hospital campus.

It had also completed the first ever delivery of medication to a retail customer. Amazon Prime Air, Walmart, and the USPS were also conducting limited tests under the watchful eye of the FAA, which has responsibility for regulating all types of drones, both recreational and commercial.

Slow Progress

Progress toward a full-scale drone delivery program has been slower than expected because the FAA imposes strict regulations on who can pilot a drone, where and when drones can fly, and what kinds of items they can carry. For example, pilots are required to be able to see their drones at all times. They are allowed to use technology such as first person view, a system that includes an onboard camera feeding a video monitor on which pilots can watch their drone. Even with that device, however, another person—a visual observer—must be able to watch the aircraft with unaided sight. Binoculars, for example, are not permitted. And both the pilot and observer are limited to flying or monitoring only one drone at a time.

FAA regulations also state that drones may only be flown during daylight hours or in twilight with appropriate anti-collision lighting. The maximum allowable altitude is 400 feet (122 m), or higher if the drone remains within 400 feet of a structure. The maximum speed allowed for a drone is 100 miles per hour (161 kph). Pilots are not allowed to fly commercial drones over anyone not directly participating in the operation, under a covered structure, or inside a covered stationary vehicle. No operations from a moving vehicle are allowed, unless the drone is flying over a sparsely populated area. Drones may carry an external load only if it is securely attached and does not adversely affect the flight characteristics or controllability of the aircraft.

Such strict regulations make it all but impossible to operate a viable drone delivery program in the United States. The only option for companies hoping to establish such programs is to convince the FAA to waive some or all of the restrictions, which would allow them to operate testing programs. Most of the companies that are doing this type of testing have sought what is known as Part 135 standard certification. Depending on the level of certification—there are four—some of the stricter FAA regulations are waived during a testing period.

Making History

In April 2019 Wing earned the first-ever Air-Carrier Certification from the FAA, allowing it to implement a consumer delivery program on a limited scale. In Christiansburg, where the Sensmeiers made history, Wing set up its operation in partnership with nearby Virginia Tech, a national leader in drone research. Under this program, customers could use an app on their phone to place an order and receive their package within about ten minutes. Wing worked with the US Department of Transportation and the FAA on what is called an Integration Pilot Program, or IPP. As part of the federal program, Wing delivered kids' snacks (goldfish, water, gummy bears, and yogurt, for example) and over-the-counter medicines such as Tylenol or cough drops from Walgreens, select packages from FedEx Express, and sweets and stationery from local retailer Sugar Magnolia. There was no delivery fee during the testing period.

autonomous

Undertaken or carried on without outside control; existing or capable of existing independently

The drone that arrived at the Sensmeiers' house departed from a base that Wing calls a nest, about a mile away. Inside, about a dozen drones sat on launchpads as their batteries were charged. Wing's drones are made of the same kind of durable foam used in bicycle helmets so they can withstand impact without causing damage. Guided by the Global Positioning System (GPS), they fly using a combination of twelve helicopter-like rotors and two wing-mounted propellers. A single pilot can monitor up to five of the autonomous aircraft from a control booth inside

How to Become a Commercial Drone Pilot

Commercial drone pilots are in high demand. The Association for Unmanned Vehicle Systems International predicts the creation of more than one hundred thousand new jobs in the unmanned aircraft industry by 2025. Drones are being tested or used in various industries, including the delivery business.

Individuals who want to work as drone pilots must obtain an FAA license. In order to obtain the license, a person must be at least sixteen years old; be able to read, speak, write, and understand English; be in a physical and mental condition to safely fly a drone; and pass the initial aeronautical knowledge exam. Although not mandatory, many pilots prepare for that test by attending a drone pilot ground school, which involves about twenty hours of instruction, study, and hands-on practice. The FAA also offers a free online course.

The written test to obtain a Remote Pilot Certificate can be taken at any FAA-approved location, usually a local flying club or airport. This test involves sixty-plus multiple-choice questions that cover setting up, operating, and safely using a drone. Test takers must answer 70 percent of the questions correctly to pass. They will also need to undergo a background check before they can obtain their Remote Pilot Certificate and begin flying.

the nest. Observers who monitor the aircraft are stationed around town. From the nest, the drone travels at speeds of up to 65 miles per hour (105 kph) and can carry 3-pound (1.4 kg) packages to delivery destinations within about 3.5 miles (5.6 km). When it arrives, the drone lowers the package and then gently releases it once it reaches the ground.

A few days after Wing delivered Susie Sensmeier's birthday present, UPS subsidiary Flight Forward also delivered what the company said was a first—prescription medication directly to a customer's home by drone. On November 1, 2019, the company flew the medication from a pharmacy in North Carolina to a customer's home before making a second delivery to a nearby

A Wing drone carries ice cream and popsicles during a demonstration delivery flight in Blacksburg, Virginia.

retirement community. The deliveries were made in partnership with CVS Pharmacy and Matternet, a drone logistics company.

Flight Forward's delivery was made autonomously but was monitored by a remote operator who was able to take over in case the drone experienced any difficulties. When it arrived, the Matternet M2 drone hovered about 20 feet (6.1 m) above the customer's property before slowly lowering its package via a cable. The hope is that drone deliveries like this will make it easier for customers with limited mobility to get their medication in the future.

Helping a Hospital

UPS had actually got its start in drone delivery a few months earlier. The company began operating a drone delivery pilot program at WakeMed Health in North Carolina in March 2019, making about fifteen hundred deliveries to facilities directly related to the hospital. What was new in the November delivery was that it included prescription medications that were flown directly to residential customers. Based on the success of the WakeMed program, UPS Flight Forward planned to expand that program to the University of Utah Health Network in Salt Lake City during 2020.

At WakeMed, UPS was also part of the same IPP as Google Wing. The companies will share data from their programs in Virginia, North Carolina, and Utah so the government can learn what works and does not work as it evaluates other drone programs. The FAA was expected to publish permanent rules on drone delivery in 2021 after analyzing the data it obtained from the program.

Amazon Plays Catch-Up

While the delivery drone frenzy in the United States began with Amazon, the company quickly fell behind Google and UPS in the race to be first. However, many industry experts believe Amazon will ultimately catch up and might possibly even exceed the reach of other drone delivery services. In the past decade, Amazon has been quietly building an army of increasingly sophisticated flying robots. Some of the drone-centered patents it filed showed a future in which drones launch from delivery trucks, trains, and ships. One patent application even showed drones being deployed from an Amazon Prime Air blimp. The company has also patented methods for syncing the drones with autonomous vehicles. One Amazon drone vision depicts a beehive-shaped fulfillment tower in a futuristic urban center, buzzing with flying robots making deliveries. Inside, robotic arms load packages onto the drones, while other robots repair damaged drones

patent

The exclusive right granted by a government to an inventor to manufacture, use, or sell an invention for a certain number of years

17

or restock shelves of inventory offloaded by autonomous trucks. The occasional human is pictured monitoring the robots.

Like Google and UPS, Amazon has also been working with regulators and industry experts to design an air traffic management system that will recognize who is flying what drone, where they are flying, and whether they are adhering to operating requirements. This system is intended to gather safety and reliability data during testing.

Walmart, Uber, and the USPS Join the Race

Retail giant Walmart has also expressed interest in becoming a player in the consumer drone delivery industry. In the near future, it hopes to test drone deliveries between its warehouses, to package pickup locations in Walmart stores, and eventually to customer's homes. Toward that end, Walmart has filed numerous patents describing systems that would safely deliver packages by drone to high-rise and medium-rise apartment buildings or offices. One patent filing was for a system that would have a

Consumers Have Mixed Views About Drone Deliveries

A 2020 survey of online shoppers found that some would order more products online if they knew their package was coming by drone, while others said this would not influence their purchase decisions. In the survey, conducted by the ratings and review platform Clutch, 39 percent said they did not care one way or the other if their packages were delivered by drone. In contrast, 36 percent said they would be more likely to order products online if they knew their purchase would be delivered by drone. The remaining 25 percent said they would be less likely to order something online if they knew it would be delivered by a drone.

Survey respondents also rated the benefits and drawbacks of drone delivery. Faster delivery times, lower costs, and reaching rural areas were among the positives. The negatives included concerns about damaged packages and hacked or stolen drones.

drone land on an outdoor platform and then send a signal that would open a trap door, enabling an automated system to move the package inside. The second filing was for a window unit including a net that would automatically catch drone deliveries, with sensors confirming the package had been dropped off.

Ride-sharing service Uber is also trying to break into the drone delivery market, specifically for bringing food directly to homes and business. Uber has even created a group devoted to on-demand air travel. Called Uber Elevate, in 2019 it unveiled a six-rotor drone capable of carrying dinner for up to two people. Its ideal trip time was eight minutes, including loading and unloading, but it could only do relatively short hauls. For example, the drone could do up to an 18-mile (29 km) trip made up of three 6-mile (9.7 km) legs: up to 6 miles to the restaurant, up to 6 miles from the restaurant to the customer, and up to 6 miles back to its launch area. The FAA granted Uber Elevate permission to operate a food delivery service by drone that was slated to begin in San Diego, California, in 2020.

Uber's initial plans, however, did not call for making food deliveries directly to customers' doors. Instead, the drones would fly to designated landing zones, which could include the roofs of parked Uber cars. Couriers would then collect the deliveries and carry them on the last leg of the journey. Uber Elevate estimated that delivering food 1.5 miles (2.4 km) via drone would take about seven minutes, compared to twenty-one minutes for the same trip via ground transportation.

The USPS joined the delivery drone competition in September 2019 when it began exploring the use of unmanned aircraft systems to supplement mail delivery on some expensive rural routes. The drones would conduct beyond-line-of-sight mail delivery to remote locations or to residences with long driveways. The drones would launch from a USPS vehicle, make their delivery, and return to the vehicle as the carrier continued along the route. The USPS also plans to offer a service that would make it possible for businesses to rent drones for their own deliveries.

Just Around the Corner

Six years after Jeff Bezos made his bold prediction, testing of consumer drone delivery services was well under way as companies searched for new ways to meet consumer demand for faster deliveries. As the delivery of Susie Sensmeier's birthday present by drone in October 2019 showed, the days of drones whizzing overhead and swooping in with packages ordered only minutes earlier might be just around the corner. "Drone delivery has the potential to radically improve the way we live by delivering products and services we need in just minutes," says Jonathan Bass, head of marketing for Google Wing. "Drones can make the transport of goods faster, safer, more efficient, sustainable and affordable, with the potential to improve the way our cities operate by reducing road congestion and creating new economic opportunities for local businesses."[7]

CHAPTER 2

Delivery Drones Around the World

Late on a Monday morning in the spring of 2018, the Chinese village of Zhangwei was quiet as usual. Chickens scratched and clucked on the side of the road, impatiently waiting to eat as workers used wooden spades to spread grain out to dry. In the heart of the village center, not far from this familiar scene that has played out for hundreds of years, there were two unmistakable signs that the country's past had caught up to its future. Visible to those present was a circle of green Astroturf laid down in the central square and a building whose sign bears the logo of Jingdong (JD), China's largest online retailer. Then, in what had become such a common occurrence that workers barely looked up, a low whirr broke the stillness. A delivery drone arrived overhead, hovered for a moment, then lowered itself toward the green circle, its three sets of propellers churning the air into small clouds of straw and dust.

Slung beneath the drone was a red cardboard box branded with JD's friendly looking dog mascot. As it hovered to within a few feet of the ground, the drone dropped its cargo, then zipped back up into the sky and quickly disappeared. The drop-off lasted no more than twenty seconds. The workers continued tending to their chores unfazed by the whole scenario that had just played out in front of them.

China Leads the Way

China began 2020 as the world leader in drone delivery of consumer goods. What set China's efforts apart from other countries' was its ability to assemble all the parts needed for drone deliveries, including compliance with government regulations, an effective infrastructure, and the world's biggest e-commerce market. Four years earlier, the Civil Aviation Administration of China (CAAC) gave the go-ahead for JD and SF Holding Co., the country's biggest express-delivery company, to start sending packages by drone in certain rural areas. The idea was for the two companies to build a network that would include not only small drones for final delivery but an entire system, including large, autonomous fixed-wing planes that would take off from small airports or landing strips to move bulk shipments between warehouses.

infrastructure

The fundamental facilities and systems serving a country, city, or area, such as transportation and communication systems, power plants, and schools

China's main incentive to quickly develop a wide-scale drone delivery program was the sheer enormity of its market—millions of consumers living in remote areas that are difficult, if not impossible, to reach by truck. For the Chinese government, leading the way in drone delivery offered a way to help alleviate poverty in rural areas and narrow the wealth gap with urban centers. It also made China a model for other governments around the world looking to draft regulations for the coming swarms of commercial drones. Promoting drone delivery was "a key opportunity for CAAC to gain a greater say in international aviation industry and overtake peers,"[8] the civil aviation administration said.

While e-commerce and delivery companies in other countries go through extensive drone delivery testing programs in hopes of meeting government standards, the Chinese government encouraged JD to take the lead in developing drones with the strength, range, and reliability to deliver goods on a large scale and solve the expensive last-mile problem. With the government's backing and few regulations to overcome, JD aggressively developed the technology necessary for successful drone deliveries starting in 2015 and began using it for deliveries in 2016, making it the first program of its kind in the world.

Since then, JD has grown its delivery network to include one hundred drone bases and seven thousand delivery centers. Zhangwei, for example, typically receives a couple of daily drops, with each box containing several packages ordered through the company's shopping app, which has more than a quarter billion registered users. Thanks to JD's fleet of drones, which operate autonomously with no human guidance but are monitored remotely, villagers in Zhangwei can expect delivery the same day they place an order for laundry detergent, phone accessories, maternity goods, fresh food, and other necessities. JD's 2/11 Promise claims that any order placed by 11:00 a.m. will be delivered by

China's civil aviation agency has given permission for the use of drones to deliver parcels in remote areas that are difficult to reach with trucks.

11:00 p.m. the same day, a goal that is met 90 percent of the time, according to the company. "People living in mountainous regions hardly accessible by ground transportation also have the right to shop," said Cui Zheng, a manager overseeing JD's drone delivery program in northwest China. "We are giving them the same shopping experience, same price, by flying drones."[9]

Providing Reliable Access to Goods

Delivering those much-needed products by drone helps the company further its vision of giving all consumers fast, reliable access to quality goods, no matter where they live. Delivering goods by drone also makes good financial sense for the company because of the rapidly growing demand for consumer products in rural areas, where more than 600 million people live and online retail sales topped $200 billion in 2019. By JD's own estimates, making a delivery by drone costs the company about one-fifth of the price of a driver and a vehicle. Liu Qiangdong, JD's chief executive, predicted drone delivery will cut costs by 70 percent once it is scaled up across the country.

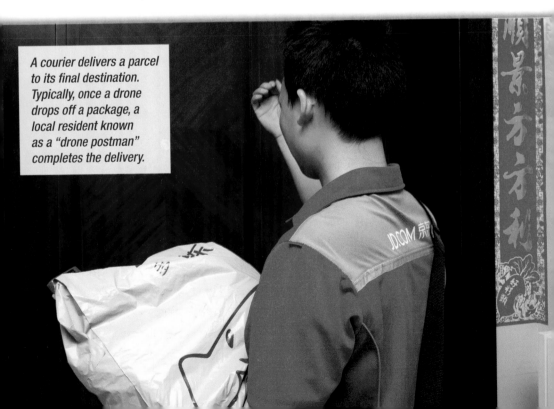

A courier delivers a parcel to its final destination. Typically, once a drone drops off a package, a local resident known as a "drone postman" completes the delivery.

In its four years of operation, JD found that drone delivery in China made sense only in rural settings. Flying in busy urban environments was too difficult for existing drone technology, although that could change in the future. For now, densely populated cities generate sufficient orders over a small area for those deliveries to be combined into daily, or even more frequent, deliveries by van. Combining sparser rural orders in the same way would result in multiday or even weeklong delivery times. For example, a round trip between JD's central warehouse and a nearby rural village usually takes about an hour for a delivery person using a three-wheeled bike. But it takes a delivery drone only six minutes to make the same trip. In one extreme case, a courier has to climb up and down a mountain for four hours to deliver a package to a village on the edge of a cliff. A drone can do the trip in minutes.

Typically, in JD's system, once the drone's cargo hits the ground, its contents pass over to the "drone postman" for delivery to customers. Sometimes this is a local JD promoter—there are about three hundred thousand across the country chosen for their familiarity with the residents and the layout of their villages—whose primary job is teaching villagers how to use the company's shopping app. Or it is a person hired on Dada, a Chinese website that matches workers with employers.

Expanding Operations

Already the dominant retailer in China, JD expanded its e-commerce operations to Indonesia in 2016, where it quickly grew to offer more than 1 million different products while serving a growing base of more than 20 million consumers. Such a massive sales operation required development of a complicated logistics network consisting of ten warehouses covering 483 cities and sixty-five hundred counties. Complicating matters was the fact that Indonesia, with the fourth-largest population in the world, comprises more than seventeen thousand islands. This made it difficult for last-mile logistics companies to deliver by road, since not all the islands are connected by bridges. JD saw drone delivery as the perfect solution, since it not only eliminated the need for expensive infrastructure to be in place for movement but also drastically cut down delivery times.

With its track record of success in drone delivery in China, JD expanded its drone operations to Indonesia in January 2019. One of the company's first drone delivery projects there was to transport a 22-pound (10 kg) package of books and backpacks about 155 miles (250 km) to students at a primary school in a village near Bandung, the country's fourth-largest city. If not for the drone, the items would have been delivered by truck over rugged roads, a slow, time-consuming, and expensive process.

It was Indonesia's first government-approved drone flight and represented a breakthrough for drone delivery in Southeast Asia. The success of this program bodes well for other countries in the region. "We have been using drones for real deliveries in China for over two years now, and have seen the profound impact this technology can have on people's lives,"[10] says Jon Liao, chief strategy officer at JD.

Alibaba Develops a Program

While JD dominated drone delivery in China and Indonesia, its chief e-commerce rival in the East, Alibaba, was slower to enter the market. Alibaba initially relied on partners to make deliveries, but then partnered with Beihang Unmanned Aircraft System to develop its own cargo drones. One model that was being worked on by the drone company was capable of carrying 1 ton (907 kg) of goods more than 932 miles (1,500 km).

In October 2017 Alibaba used drones to deliver packages over a body of water for the first time. Three drones carrying six boxes of passion fruit with a combined weight of around 26 pounds (12 kg) flew from Fujian Province in eastern China to nearby Meizhou Island. Flying into a strong wind, the drones took nine minutes to make the 3-mile (5 km) crossing. Zeng Jinmei, an online store owner based on the island, said that the

Global Drone Delivery Guidelines

In January 2019 the World Economic Forum released a report called The Advanced Drone Operations Toolkit: Accelerating the Drone Revolution. This is a set of guidelines, recommendations, and lessons learned for governments looking to roll out commercial drone operations. It was developed with the assistance of government agencies and private companies worldwide.

The tool kit offers help in many areas, including suggestions for crafting reasonable safety regulations. The goal is to avoid rules that prevent steady progress but still account for safety needs. The information contained in the tool kit has been gathered from the experiences of existing drone delivery projects. It is a sort of It blueprint that can be adapted to meet each country's needs. "Now, governments can learn from the real-world success of world-leading drone delivery projects in Africa and Europe to develop their own national oversight," says report author Harrison Wolf.

Quoted in Greg Nichols, "Davos Develops Drone Regulation How-To for Governments (and the FAA Should Pay Attention)," ZDNet, January 28, 2019. www.zdnet.com.

drone delivery service would cut transportation time by half and save operating costs.

Delivery Drones in Other Countries

While China was the world leader in drone delivery of consumer products at the start of 2020, companies in twenty-six other nations around the world were in various stages of drone testing programs. A few—in France, Finland, Iceland, Australia, and Singapore—were looking to grow their already established but limited drone delivery operations.

In December 2019 the French postal service, La Poste, began delivering packages by drone to remote villages. By using drones, the postal operator was able to keep up a regular service even in winter, when heavy snowfall often makes access to villages in the mountains difficult. The service began in the small village of

Fontanil-Cornillon, where the operator parked his truck and flew the drone containing the packages up the mountain to the small village of Mont-Saint-Martin, 2,493 feet (760 m) above sea level. The package was then deposited into a secure terminal, and the recipient received a code by text to collect it. The drone flew at around 19 miles per hour (30 kph) and could complete the round trip in about eight minutes, saving time as well as reducing traffic congestion on the narrow mountain roads. "In the Alps, snow falls regularly in these mountain areas and can prevent a traditional delivery person from climbing to Mont-Saint-Martin. Thanks to the drone, we will still be able to transport the packages to the village,"[11] Jean-Luc Defrance, director of drones and autonomous vehicles at the French parcel delivery service DPD Groupe, told a reporter.

Even as it continued to test a delivery program in the United States, Google Wing was also looking toward other countries for drone delivery opportunities. It launched a trial delivery service in Finland's capital, Helsinki, in June 2019. Those flights covered a maximum of 6.2 miles (10 km) in about ten minutes with packages weighing 3.3 pounds (1.5 kg) or less. Wing began its service by offering products from two shops, a gourmet supermarket and a local restaurant, to residents in the city's Vuosaari district. Wing users could order lasagna for two; a chicken Caesar salad; a classic home movie combo of popcorn, candy, and soda from the Food Market Herkku; or items ranging from a salmon sandwich to a Portuguese sweet custard tart from Cafe Monami, a popular dining spot among locals.

Wing chose Vuosaari in part because of its geographic location. The district is bordered by water on three sides, has significant forestland alongside residential areas, and features a large international cargo port. These features meant fewer potential obstacles and thus greater safety in flight. The density of Vuosaari's population also made it a great place to launch the service to multifamily housing communities. Wing's drone delivery program coincided with Helsinki's stated goal of making cars obsolete by 2025. The efficiency of drone delivery would mean fewer cars making trips for small purchases.

Google Wing Flies in Australia

While Finland marked Wing's first program in Europe, it was the company's second extended pilot program outside the United States. The company also ran four separate trials covering some fifty-five thousand journeys in Australia, carrying products as diverse as medicine and coffee across a range of environments. Despite complaints from residents about excessive noise, the Civil Aviation Safety Authority (CASA) granted Wing approval to launch a public drone delivery service in Canberra starting in April 2019. About one hundred homes in three suburban communities were given access to the service.

Wing predicted that drone deliveries could be worth as much as $30 million to $40 million to businesses in the area and that drones could deliver as many as one in four orders by 2030. The company partnered with several local businesses, including coffee shops and pharmacies, to deliver their products in minutes.

cocoon

A protective covering placed over a product to keep it safe during transportation

Coffee is a popular item among Wing's customers in Canberra. It is not an item typically delivered by car because of how quickly it gets cold. In the drone, it travels in a normal to-go cup and is protected by a recyclable paper cocoon. "Our record is 3 minutes and 17 seconds from an order to coffee in hand,"[12] says Wing CEO James Burgess.

CASA's approval came with some operational restrictions. Drones are not allowed to fly over main roads and can only fly during specified hours. They are also restricted from flying too close to people. Customers in eligible homes were also given a safety briefing about interacting with the drones.

Drones in Iceland

Drone delivery arrived in Iceland in 2017. That year one of the country's largest e-commerce companies (called Aha) began using a Chinese-made drone and an Israeli logistics system to deliver hot food, groceries, and electronics to households within a 5-mile (8-km) radius in the capital city of Reykjavik. A delivery can be completed in as little as four minutes, versus twenty-five minutes by car or truck in heavy traffic. Aha's drone delivery service operates until 7:00 p.m. in Reykjavik on days that are not too windy, snowy, or rainy.

Aha's system is unique in that its drones are not fitted with any sensors to avoid obstacles, nor do they have cameras, radar, or any other imaging systems. They fly according to GPS coordinates, along thirteen main flight paths that have been certified free of trees, buildings, and other impediments. Everything a drone passes over, including roads and buildings, has been put into a geographic model that assesses the risk to people if a 34-pound (15.4 kg) drone were to come crashing to earth.

Initially, the drones arrived at a dozen or so set drop-off points with a company representative designated to receive the drone and pull the package out of a cargo compartment. Later, the company received permission to lower packages on a line to about one thousand select homes. These drops have

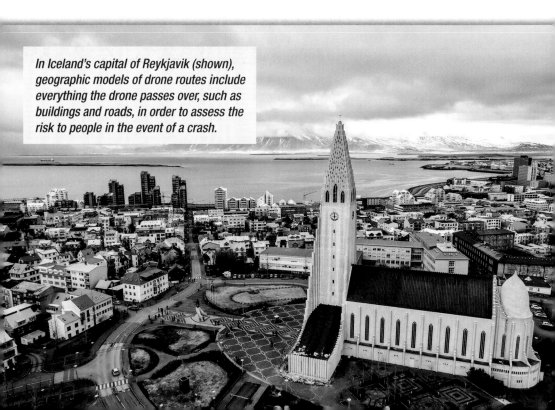

In Iceland's capital of Reykjavik (shown), geographic models of drone routes include everything the drone passes over, such as buildings and roads, in order to assess the risk to people in the event of a crash.

Fighting Coronavirus with Drones

Drones played an important role in fighting the spread of the Covid-19 coronavirus in China in 2020. Crop-spraying drones equipped with disinfectant were dispatched to Shandong Province, for example. The Chinese agricultural technology company XAG sent a fleet of drones to spray disinfectant in Shandong Province. The company said its fleet covered almost 359,000 square yards (300,000 sq. m) in less than four hours. One enterprising villager in the same province even repurposed his own drones to spray disinfectant around his village spanning about 19,000 square yards (16,000 sq. m).

Local and provincial governments found other uses for drones. Some mounted megaphones on drones, which were then used to disperse public gatherings and scold people who were not wearing masks. In Shanghai, officials deployed drones to monitor workers who were stopping travelers for temperature checks. And, in Zhongshan, drones were used to oversee the disposal of hospital medical waste.

Drones also provided an important service in Wuhan, the epicenter of the outbreak. During construction of two temporary hospitals, six large drones hovered 164 feet (50 m) above ground to provide light for workers toiling around the clock.

proved to be very accurate. "It can drop a package almost on a carpet in your backyard,"[13] says Yariv Bash of Flytrex, an Israeli logistics firm.

Drones in Canada

With so many remote areas that are difficult to reach by normal means of transportation, Canada is a prime candidate for drone delivery programs. In November 2019 Toronto-based Drone Delivery Canada (DDC) formed a partnership with Air Canada and the Edmonton (Alberta) International Airport. The partnership's goal is the creation of the world's first airport-based drone-delivery hub that would serve multiple drone delivery companies.

DDC has built its reputation on its deliveries of supplies to remote parts of Canada. DDC's Sparrow X1000 cargo drone, guided by its proprietary FLYTE management system, has been used for transport of medical supplies, food, automotive parts, and other items.

In February 2019 DDC unveiled its largest and longest-range drone, the Condor. Unlike most other battery-powered drones, the single-rotor Condor is powered by a gas engine and can carry up to 400 pounds (181 kg) over a distance of up to 124 miles (200 km). The Condor measures 22 feet (6.7 m) long and is about 5 feet (1.5 m) wide and 7 feet (2.1 m) tall. It has a wing-span of approximately 20 feet (6.1 m) and is capable of vertical takeoff and landing.

payload

The goods that are transported by planes, usually expressed by weight

DDC also planned to use its smaller Sparrow drones to deliver medicine, food, and mail in 2020 to about five thousand residents of a remote First Nation island in northern Ontario. Under the plan, DDC was to transport goods from the mainland town of Moosonee to Moose Factory Island, which is only accessible by boat in summer, frozen waterways in winter, and helicopter at other times. Drones were expected to have an 11-pound (5 kg) maximum payload for the roughly ten-minute journey across the Moose River.

The project was the first in DDC's remote communities initiative with plans to grow over the next few years. DDC estimated that Canada has about one thousand such remote communities facing infrastructure and logistics challenges. "It's really about trying to service communities that lack infrastructure, where basic goods are very difficult to obtain, and when you can obtain them, it is very, very expensive,"[14] says Tony Di Benedetto, the head of DDC.

CHAPTER 3

Designing the Perfect Drone

For two years, the Swiss Post, Switzerland's equivalent to the USPS, operated a drone delivery program in three cities. The drones flawlessly delivered lab samples between hospitals, clinics, and laboratories through more than three thousand flights. Then, twice in a matter of months during 2019, one of its quadcopter drones suffered a catastrophic failure.

The worst accident happened in May, when one of the 22-pound (10 kg) drones operated by US start-up Matternet on behalf of the Swiss Post, encountered an issue during a flight. It crashed near Zurich University while carrying nearly 5 pounds (2.3 kg) of cargo. A group of kindergarten children were playing just 50 yards (46 m) from where the drone landed, unaware of what had just happened. Even though the drone was equipped with an emergency parachute system in case of such an in-air incident, the cord connecting the parachute to the drone was severed, resulting in an uncontrolled crash. Fortunately, no one on the ground was injured. Four months earlier, another Matternet drone suffered an issue with its GPS system, likely a short circuit that interrupted the power supply, causing it to make an emergency landing. However, in that case the drone's parachute successfully deployed, and the landing was controlled.

In response to the two crashes, the Swiss Post required Matternet to make several changes to the safety features of its drones. For example, each drone has to be connected to its parachute by two cords rather than one. Those cords must also be reinforced with metal braiding, and the emergency landing whistle must be louder to give people on the ground earlier warning that a drone is out of control.

mechanism
A system of parts working together in a machine

Matternet officials said that they had never seen a failure like the one that its drone experienced in May and that the drone's parachute system had never failed before. "A failure of the parachute system is a clear failure of our safety mechanisms and we are taking all the appropriate measures to address it,"[15] the company said. It vowed to restart operations only after a fix had been made.

After making the required improvements, Swiss Post's drone delivery program resumed in January 2020. A group of independent aviation experts took a close look at the built-in safety mechanisms of the Matternet drones and the improvements required by Swiss government officials. As a group, the experts certified that Swiss Post and Matternet maintain high safety standards and a high level of safety awareness. They said processes that were examined were at a high standard even before the incidents. They also said there were no reasons why flight operations should not be resumed.

Making Safety a Priority

Those two incidents highlighted the challenges engineers face in developing drone delivery systems. Drones have to be lightweight but still strong enough to fly in difficult weather conditions such as wind, snow, and rain. They must have powerful batteries that are capable of extended flight time but not so bulky that they take up a lot of space. They need sophisticated sensors to detect and avoid obstacles. They need precision guidance systems to allow them to have pinpoint accuracy in finding a delivery location. And they must have a foolproof way of releasing packages at their final destination.

But most of all, drones need to be designed in such a way as to ensure the safety of people on the ground. Unpredictable weather, finicky technology, buildings and trees, other aircraft, and even flocks of birds pose significant challenges for engineers to overcome. Each of the major players in the drone delivery industry has come up with its own creative solutions to these practical problems.

Companies interested in entering the drone delivery race have two choices: rely on an already established drone maker, such as Matternet or DJI, or design their own drone. Either way, it requires huge teams of workers with sophisticated engineering skills and technological expertise, plus the ability to solve difficult problems through creative problem solving, exhaustive testing, and team-work to come up with the most effective solutions. Such a pro-cess is expensive and time consuming.

Those who design drones that operate over populated areas must work to ensure the safety of people on the ground.

Amazon's team tried out roughly fifty thousand concepts before settling on its latest design, a hybrid drone. It has a vertical takeoff and landing capability similar to a helicopter. But it is also capable of sustained forward flight like a fixed-wing aircraft. Amazon's hexagonal wings help stabilize the drone in gusty winds and double as a shield to protect the six propellers, two key factors in operational safety. The drone uses a combination of thermal cameras, depth cameras, and sonar to detect hazards. With the help of machine-learning models, Amazon's drones can automatically identify obstacles and navigate around them.

Onboard computers keep a lookout for objects that might get in the way as the drone descends, using a combination of stereo vision and artificial intelligence algorithms trained to detect people and animals from above. While introducing the drone at Amazon's re:MARS conference in Las Vegas in June 2019, Amazon's Worldwide Consumer division CEO Jeff Wilke emphasized the aircraft's safety features. "We know customers will only feel comfortable receiving drone deliveries if the system is incredibly safe,"[16] said Wilke.

One feature that differentiates Amazon's drones from others in the industry is something called six degrees of freedom. This is the ability of an object to move forward/backward, up/down, and left/right combined with rotation around three perpendicular axes, often termed pitch, yaw, and roll. Six degrees of freedom allows for more dynamic and nimble flight, a key factor in dealing with unexpected weather

hybrid

Formed or composed of two or more unlike elements

machine learning

The algorithms and statistical models that computer systems use to perform specific tasks without using explicit instructions, relying on patterns and inference instead

Managing Drone Traffic

In February 2019 the FAA chose the Mid-Atlantic Aviation Partnership (MAAP) at Virginia Tech as one of three test sites for a new program focused on managing drone traffic. As the use of drones becomes more prevalent, there will be a need to control traffic, much the same way air traffic controllers manage airplane traffic. Flight planning, weather services, and communications fall under what the drone industry calls unmanned aircraft system traffic management, or UTM. The UTM Pilot Program is designed to move these technologies from research and testing to everyday use. "Managing drone traffic means solving a whole set of complicated problems simultaneously," says MAAP director Mark Blanks. "Now, we're seeing this work come to fruition as technology that has the potential to dramatically expand the industry."

The tests, which began in 2019, incorporated traffic management systems from four companies. The ability for software from different providers to interact seamlessly is critical: for a variety of drones performing a range of missions to share the airspace safely, they must be able to communicate fluently. UTM is the medium for those interactions.

Quoted in Eleanor Nelsen, "Selection for Drone Traffic-Management Program Reflects Virginia's Leadership in UAS Integration," Virginia Tech, February 25, 2019. https://vtnews.vt.edu.

changes such as heavy rain or wind. A tilting design allows for the drone to use the same six propellers to fly forward as it does for takeoff and landing. Its propellers are optimized to reduce high-frequency sounds, the annoying whirring that draws frequent complaint from people on the ground about drone deliveries. Packages are carried in the middle of the fuselage for delivery.

Google's Drone Concept

Google Wing is also working with its own drone design. One challenge has been finding a way to extend flying time. To do this, Wing engineers have reduced the drone's weight and improved its aerodynamics.

Wing's H-shaped drone looks more like a small plane than a traditional drone. It has two wings, each extending more than 3 feet (91.4 cm), and a propeller. This allows the drone to fly faster—up to 75 miles per hour (120 kph), driven by an energy-efficient, all-electric power system with zero carbon emissions. Altogether, the drone has fourteen propellers specifically designed to minimize noise, an important feature if the drones are to be used in residential areas. Wing began drone trials in Australia in 2017 and has conducted more than eighty thousand tests.

To start the delivery process, Wing's drone is designed to hover in the air while it picks up a package from a distribution center, sending a tether down so a worker can attach the payload. The drones' route is mapped out by Wing's Unmanned Aircraft System Traffic Management (UTM) platform, which allocates flight paths and makes sure aircraft are able to follow routes that avoid each other, buildings, trees and other hazards.

Wing's delivery drone never actually lands. Instead, once the drone reaches a customer's home, a tether lowers a box to the ground from about 24 feet (7.3 m) in the air and automatically unclips the package. The company designed the tether to create a safe space between its drone and customers and spent hundreds of hours coming up with a hook system that easily releases the package.

UPS Partners with Matternet

Not all companies involved in the drone delivery industry are designing and building their own drones. Drone design and construction can be expensive and time consuming; it also requires specialized expertise. These are among the reasons why UPS Flight Forward has partnered with drone manufacturer Matternet for its drone delivery program.

Together, UPS and Matternet established the first FAA-approved drone airline, which began in March 2019 at WakeMed Health in Raleigh, North Carolina. The Matternet M2 drone's logistics system operates on the company's Cloud Platform. This

The delivery company UPS has partnered with the drone manufacturer Matternet and CVS Pharmacy to create a system for delivering prescription drugs to consumers.

platform receives customer requests, generates routes, and monitors, commands, and controls all operating Matternet drones. The M2 is capable of transporting packages up to 5 pounds (2.3 kg) over distances of up to 12.5 miles (20 km) in operations beyond visual line of sight and over people.

For a typical flight at WakeMed in 2019, a medical professional loaded a secure drone container with a medical sample or specimen—such as a blood sample—at one of the hospital system's nearby facilities. The drone flew along a predetermined flight path, monitored by a specially trained remote pilot, to a fixed landing pad at WakeMed's main hospital and central pathology lab.

How Uber Eats Will Deliver Food

Uber Eats, an offshoot of the ride-sharing service, began testing drone delivery in 2019. Using special delivery packages that keep burgers and fries hot and intact during flight, Uber Eats completed limited tests of commercial food delivery by drone in May 2019. The tests took place at a McDonald's restaurant in San Diego, California.

But Uber Eats was not using drones for store-to-door delivery. Once a customer placed a food order, the restaurant prepared the meal and then loaded it onto a drone. That drone then flew to a predetermined drop-off location or landing zone. Using a light-weight computing platform with 4G cellular connectivity, the Uber Eats drone can maintain a flight path when out of sight of the pilot. Behind the scenes, Uber's Elevate Cloud Services tracked and guided the drone and notified an Eats delivery driver when and where to pick up the food.

With the help of parachutes attached to the drones, Uber experimented with landing on mailboxes and in backyards. But in urban areas, where backyards and street-level mailboxes are less common, such landing sites could be hard to find. Another possible option for urban areas was to have the drones land on top of parked Uber vehicles. These would be identified with QR codes

The food delivery service Uber Eats is considering using drones to deliver meals to the drivers of parked Uber vehicles, who would then complete the delivery to the consumer.

located near the delivery location. From there, the Eats delivery driver would hand deliver the food to the customer. "We don't need to get the drone direct to our customers or consumers," says Luke Fischer, head of flight operations for Uber Elevate. "We just have to get it close enough."[17]

The San Diego trials provided Uber Elevate valuable information about how to manage this new aerial infrastructure. The company expects to establish regular deliveries in a handful of markets by the mid-2020s. It has also predicted that drone deliveries will be so prevalent within ten years that fast-food restaurants will redesign their kitchens around them.

At the start of 2020, Uber Elevate unveiled a new drone of its own design for use by Uber Eats. This drone uses innovative rotating wings with six rotors to better enable the transition between vertical takeoff and forward flight. Rotating wings were more commonly seen in flying car prototypes such as Uber's aerial taxi than in drones. In the new design, the rotors are positioned vertically for takeoff and landing but can rotate into the forward position for increased speed and efficiency during flight. The cargo capacity for the Uber drone is a meal for two.

Uber's drone was designed to perform a maximum delivery leg in eight minutes, including loading and unloading, with a total flight range of 18 miles (29 km) without a delivery and 12 miles (19.3 km) with a delivery. And the drone could hover in wind speeds up to 30 miles per hour (48 kph), making it possible to carry out deliveries in less-than-ideal weather conditions.

Finding the Right Delivery Spot

One of the biggest questions with drone delivery, according to experts, is figuring out the best place to drop off the package. Drones might solve the last-mile problem of a delivery, but the "last fifty feet" is still another significant challenge. "The best experience for the customer is their package gracefully drifting down from the sky and landing right where they want it," says Ryan Oksenhorn, cofounder of Zipline International. "To do this, we needed to engineer solutions to quite a few hard problems,"[18] including wind.

Most companies proposed to solve the issue using parachutes or tethers, but as Uber Eats discovered, finding places to land in busy urban areas can be challenging. Amazon filed a patent to use street lamps for drone delivery stations. DHL's Parcelcopter drops packages at a "smart locker" and sends recipients a code to unlock it. And in 2019 Matternet developed a van-top landing pad for delivery drones.

One delivery solution envisioned by Walmart involves a drone landing on a platform outside a building. When the drone lands, it sends a signal to the platform letting it know the package has been delivered, which then opens a trap door. The patent application says a "transportation system" would then move the pack-

Tracking Drones

As the use of drones increases, the number of reported incidents of near-collisions with other aircraft is also on the rise. In January 2020, for example, a medical helicopter pilot said he passed within 100 feet (30 m) of a drone while out on a routine medical call near Fort Morgan, Colorado. It was not an isolated incident. The FAA says it received 2,150 incident reports of drones coming too close to aircraft in 2019.

No accidents have been reported. However, in response to incidents like these, and other possible drone threats, law enforcement and Homeland Security agencies have demanded a tracking system for drones. Under proposed FAA regulations, all delivery drones would be required to broadcast their in-flight position and operator identity. The tracking system would resemble the existing air traffic control system for traditional aircraft. Only the smallest civilian drones would be exempt from the rules. "This is an important building block in the unmanned traffic management ecosystem," says the FAA.

Quoted in Alan Levin, "FAA: Drones Need Huge Tracking Network for Expanded Flights," *Lewiston (ID) Tribune*, January 5, 2020. https://lmtribune.com.

age from the outside of the building to the interior, perhaps via some sort of slide. Walmart filed another patent that outlined a slightly simpler solution for its drone delivery system. This one is a window unit that includes a frame holding a net where the drone could drop packages. Sensors would then confirm the delivery of the package.

Companies such as Amazon, Google, UPS, and Uber have come a long way in developing drone delivery programs that work under controlled situations. However, many challenges remain. Only after all these problems are solved will drones be delivering last-minute packages or breakfast burritos on doorsteps.

CHAPTER 4

Delivering Health and Saving Lives

Two-year-old Ghislane Ihimbazwe was near death when she arrived by ambulance at a hospital in central Rwanda in December 2016. In the preceding days she had shown signs of an especially virulent form of malaria. Her symptoms included high fever and pain that was severe enough to make her scream. Her mother had at first taken her to a local medical clinic but staff there did not have the tools to help her. They suggested she be transferred to a hospital. By the time Ghislane and her mother reached the hospital by ambulance, however, the little girl's condition was dire. "We arrived too late," the girl's mother said. "There was no sign of life. I thought she was dead."[19]

Hospital staff took one look at the little girl and realized that the malaria was attacking her red blood cells. They immediately recommended a blood transfusion. But there was a problem. The nearest blood bank with the needed blood supplies was an hour and a half away by car. The trip there and back would take at least three hours—and the hospital staff knew that little Ghislane did not have that much time.

Out of desperation, a hospital lab technician decided to take a chance on a new method of delivery. He typed out the order and sent it by phone. Almost immediately, he received confirmation that the blood would arrive at the hospital within six minutes.

As promised, the life-saving blood supplies reached the hospital within minutes. It arrived in an insulated cardboard box attached to a paper parachute that had been dropped from a drone. The blood was rushed to the emergency department, where Ghislane clung to life. Hospital staff sprung into action, immediately starting the transfusion. The drone delivery proved to be the miracle Ghislane's mother had desperately hoped for. Her daughter survived— and in the process, she became the first known person in the world whose life had been saved by a medical drone delivery.

intravenous

Administered through a vein, usually medicine or blood

Making Healthcare Accessible

It was a welcome sign of things to come in the rapidly evolving world of delivery drones. Drones have been especially useful for delivering medical supplies, blood products, and medicines to people in countries where access to healthcare services often is limited by the terrain. By late 2019 delivery drones had begun to make a significant difference in the lives of sick Africans. Supported by a complex logistics system, drones have flown more than 621,371 miles (1 million km) and carried out twenty-four thousand deliveries—about one-third of them when someone's life was on the line—and provided access to urgently needed medicine to more than 16 million people in Africa.

The drone that delivered Ghislane's lifesaving blood was designed and operated by Zipline International, which was founded by Harvard graduate and former professional rock climber Keller Rinaudo. Based in San Francisco, California, Zipline was born in 2014 as an innovative medical product delivery company. Part of Rinaudo's motivation for starting Zipline was to meet the need for medical care in underserved areas like Africa. "If we're going to have instant delivery for hamburgers, we should absolutely have instant delivery for medicine,"[20] says Rinaudo.

Zipline says its goal is to "provide every human on Earth with instant access to vital medical supplies."[21] Zipline plans to expand service to 700 million people by 2024 by operating in developed

An employee of the medical product delivery company Zipline prepares a drone to carry blood supplies to a clinic in a remote location.

and developing countries across Africa, Latin America, South Asia, and Southeast Asia. As of May 2019, more than 65 percent of all blood deliveries in Rwanda used Zipline drones. These have replaced cars and trucks that would have needed to travel by a treacherously tangled road network, losing precious hours in the race to save lives.

Blood is one of the most vital elements of modern medicine. Without it, major surgery would be impossible, car accidents more deadly, and the risk of death in childbirth exponentially higher. In large portions of Africa, hospitals do not have the budget—or even the electricity—to maintain their own refrigerated blood banks. While Rwanda's maternal mortality rate is improving, it is still twenty times worse than that of the United States, mostly because of severe bleeding after childbirth. According to Rwanda's Ministry of Health, nearly half of all the units of blood delivered nationwide by Zipline are for complications in childbirth.

Serving an Urgent Need

Zipline's arrival in Rwanda made a dramatic difference for one Rwandan maternity ward that saw an average of ten births a day.

At least a third of these were cesarean sections that required blood transfusion. At least twice a week, there was an urgent case for which there was not enough blood on hand or not the right type of blood for the patient.

Thanks to Zipline, drone deliveries kept the Nyanza Hospital lab stocked with sufficient amounts of blood most of the time. When he first heard his hospital would be using Zipline to deliver blood, Dr. Roger Nyonzima was incredulous. "I knew there were drones for surveillance, and I knew that militaries use them to kill enemies, but I didn't know that drones could save lives," says Nyonzima, head surgeon at Nyanza Hospital's maternity ward. "Now I don't care how the blood comes, as long as it comes in 15 minutes."[22]

In addition to its impact on lifesaving emergencies, Zipline's drone delivery service helped transform the country's medical supply chain by ensuring timely replenishment of products. In April 2019 the government of Rwanda expanded its partnership with Zipline by adding 169 additional critical and lifesaving medical products, including emergency vaccines, routine vaccines, and essential medical supplies, to its delivery program. The service operates twenty-four hours a day, seven days a week, from two distribution centers—each equipped with thirty drones—and makes deliveries to two thousand health facilities. By the end of 2019, Zipline drones were completing up to six hundred on-demand delivery flights a day, although each drone has the capacity to make up to five hundred flights per day. In addition to ensuring hospitals always have access to blood products, Zipline drones have also reduced waste and spoilage by over 95 percent by providing more timely and reliable service.

Expanding to Ghana

Because of its success in Rwanda, Zipline also began operating in Ghana, a West African nation of 29 million people, in 2019. The company opened four distribution centers serving people in locations from the densely populated southern regions surrounding the capital city of Accra to the remote and arid area in the northern part of the country. About 45 percent of Ghanaians live in rural areas, according to World Bank data, and they suffer from a higher incidence of diseases such as malaria than do urban Ghanaians. Although malaria is preventable and curable, rural Ghanaians often lack timely access to the treatments that could save their lives. That is why Zipline's presence inspired so much hope. The drone program "represents a major step toward giving everyone in this country universal access to lifesaving medicine," says Ghana's President Nana Akufo-Addo. "No one in Ghana should die because they can't access the medicine they need in an emergency."[23]

The expansion of Zipline's operations in Ghana and Rwanda increased the number of its health facilities in Africa by almost one hundred times. In only six months Zipline went from one distribution center in one country delivering blood to twenty-one hospitals to operating six distribution centers in two countries delivering more than 170 different vaccines, blood products, and medications to

The president of Ghana, Nana Akufo-Addo, hailed the decision by Zipline to expand its delivery service to include his nation.

twenty-five hundred health facilities serving close to 22 million people. Zipline's commercial partnerships with Ghana and Rwanda are expected to help save tens of thousands of lives. The rapid delivery of blood, vaccines, medications, and other medical supplies right to where they are needed could help stop outbreaks of life-threatening communicable diseases.

communicable

Capable of being easily transmitted

Serving the South Pacific

The use of drones to deliver critical medical supplies is not limited to Africa. By the end of 2019, drones had become an essential tool for delivering vaccines to people living in the South Pacific country of Vanuatu, which is made up of eighty-two small islands stretched out over 808 miles (1,300 km). Typically, one in five children living on these islands misses out on their critical childhood vaccinations due to the difficulty of getting the medicine to them. With many areas accessible only by foot or local boat, the rugged terrain presents a challenge in transporting vaccines, which must be maintained at specific temperatures and can become damaged by Vanuatu's tropical climate.

With financial support from the United Nations Children's Fund (UNICEF), the Australian government, and the Global Fund to Fight AIDS, Tuberculosis and Malaria, Vanuatu's Ministry of Health and its Civil Aviation Authority began using drones to supply vaccines to the country's outlying islands. Carried in Styrofoam boxes, vaccines are packaged among ice packs to keep them cool and are monitored by a sensor that is automatically triggered if the vaccines reach too high a temperature. The drones, operated by Australian start-up Swoop Aero, are capable of maintaining an altitude of 500 feet (152 m) in the hot, tropical climate and can fly in rain and winds up to 30 miles an hour (48 kph). They can be piloted from anywhere in the world, using a satellite network to communicate with operators on the ground, and are able to fly even if local mobile networks malfunction.

In December 2018 UNICEF claimed that one-month-old Joy Nowai from Vanuatu was the world's first child to receive a drone-delivered vaccine. Miriam Nampil, the nurse who delivered the history-making vaccine, recalled earlier times when she carried ice-filled boxes to keep the vaccines cool while walking across rivers, over mountains, through the rain, and across rocky ledges. She relied on boats, which were often canceled due to bad weather. Because the journey was so long and difficult, she

A Flying Medical Toolbox

In a medical emergency, the response time can be the difference between life and death. Unfortunately, ambulances typically arrive about ten minutes after the emergency call has been made. In those precious minutes, a cardiac arrest victim may succumb to a lack of oxygen to the brain.

At the end of 2019, engineers at Delft University of Technology in the Netherlands were working on an ambulance drone that would be dispatched to help cardiac arrest victims. Essentially a compact flying medical toolbox, the drone would deliver a built-in automated external defibrillator (AED) and live web camera with audio so professionals could instruct bystanders on how to start cardiopulmonary resuscitation and use the AED to restore a normal heart rhythm before first responders arrive on the scene.

The current prototype is able to reach patients within one minute in a 4.6-square-mile (12 sq. km) grid. Flying autonomously, it can locate the patient using GPS coordinates. With a carbon-composite chassis to reduce weight, the drone weighs in at 8.8 pounds (4 kg) and can carry its own weight in payload.

Delft University of Technology graduate student Alec Momont, the ambulance drone's designer, says, "Currently, only 20% of untrained people are able to successfully apply a defibrillator. This rate can be increased to 90% if people are provided with instructions at the scene. Moreover, the presence of the emergency operator via the drone's loudspeaker helps to reduce the panic of the situation."

Quoted in Connex Drones, "Ambulance Drones—Saving Lives," February 20, 2019. https://connexdrones .com.

often made it out only once a month to vaccinate children. "But now, with these drones, we can hope to reach many more children in the remotest areas of the island,"[24] she says.

Small, Rural Hospitals Are Closing

Delivery drones could become a critical part of healthcare in the United States as well, according to Rinaudo. Zipline plans to launch drone delivery programs to serve rural communities in Maryland, Nevada, and Washington, where access to hospital services can be difficult. "People think what we do is solving a developing economies problem. But critical-access hospitals are closing at an alarming rate in the U.S., too, especially if you live in the rural U.S. Life expectancy there has declined over the past several years,"[25] Rinaudo says.

critical-access hospital

A small, usually rural hospital that likely would be closed if not for federal subsidies

North Carolina has also provided a testing ground for drones carrying medical supplies. In August 2018 WakeMed Health and Hospitals in Raleigh, North Carolina, teamed up with the North Carolina Department of Transportation's Division of Aviation to conduct a first round of test flights for drones to carry simulated medical packages short distances. Testing went so well that in March 2019 the hospital partnered with Matternet and UPS to deliver medical samples and specimens to buildings across the WakeMed campus. Deliveries begin with a medical professional loading a secure drone container with a medical sample or specimen—such as a blood sample—at one of WakeMed's nearby facilities. From there, the drone flies along a flight path predetermined by Matternet's cloud software. In case of a midflight problem, the drone is monitored by a specially trained remote pilot stationed at a fixed landing pad at WakeMed's main hospital and central pathology lab. Stuart Ginn, medical director of WakeMed Innovations, says the use of drones will provide an option for on-demand and same-day delivery of samples, furnish the ability to avoid roadway delays, increase medical delivery efficiency, and lower costs. "In healthcare, that translates directly into patient care,"[26] Ginn says.

Designing Hospitals for Drones

Because of the potential positive impacts of integrating drones into patient care programs, some hospital designers are already imagining a future in which drones will be a major part of the daily routine of a healthcare facility. Leo A Daly, a Miami-based architecture firm, has been working on a concept for a hospital designed to allow drones to deliver food and medical supplies to patients from off-site facilities. This would allow for smaller hospitals, which could in turn lead to significant savings in construction and staffing costs.

The Daly firm's plans envisioned each patient room being outfitted with a drone

integrating

The process of uniting or combining

A Delivery Drone in the Smithsonian

The National Air and Space Museum in Washington, DC, displays many mile-stones of aviation history. In 2016 it added the first delivery drone to its exhibits. The drone on display was a Flirtey F3.0 hexacopter used to deliver twenty-four medical packages from a nearby airfield to a medical clinic in Wise, Virginia, in 2015. The fight, which covered about a half-mile (.8 km) each way and took just over six minutes, is believed to be the first legal drone delivery made in the United States. A few months later, the same drone completed another first, a ship-to-shore delivery of medical specimens across the Delaware Bay between a barge floating off the New Jersey coast and the Cape May-Lewes Ferry Termi-nal. As a result of those two history-making flights, the Flirtey drone has joined other milestones of aviation history at the museum.

delivery port on the outside of the hospital. A cargo net would receive deliveries, which would then be slid into the room and stored in a moisture- and tamper-free cabinet to be retrieved later. Daly was in talks with hospitals in Puerto Rico to install delivery ports on buildings being rebuilt after Hurricane Maria ravaged the island in 2017.

Drones in an Emergency

Drone deliveries are not limited to items such as blood and vac-cines. In September 2019 Nevada-based drone company Flirtey and the city of Reno were among ten sites chosen for the FAA and US Department of Transportation's unmanned aircraft system Integration Pilot Program (IPP). Within the IPP, Flirtey and the city have partnered with the Reno Emergency Medical Services Au-thority to deliver automated external defibrillators (AEDs) to those in need. Using historical data, Flirtey estimated that just one of its drones carrying AEDs and operating in an area with the population density of Reno will save one life every two weeks. If the services expanded across the country, it could save about 150,000 lives a year. Eventually, drones could also carry other emergency medical supplies. "I could see delivery of EpiPens for people having an allergic reaction while they're out for lunch," says Flirtey's CEO, Matt Sweeney. "I could see delivery of Narcan in the event of an opioid overdose. Seeing a Flirtey drone delivering an AED will be as common as seeing an ambulance on the road."[27]

Drones were also becoming valuable tools on military battlefields. Researchers at the US Army's Telemedicine & Advanced Technology Research Center were collaborating with other military branches, research and development universities, and private industry to develop drones capable of bringing medical supplies straight to soldiers wounded in combat. From blood products to bandages and sutures, delivering these products directly to the area where a soldier has been injured could one day prove vital for the successful work of field medics. Inaccessible terrain and enemy threats often make it impossible to move a wounded soldier to a medical base quickly or efficiently, and in conditions like these, drone delivery could be lifesaving.

Drones are saving lives. Whether it is by delivering blood for a young girl in Rwanda, vaccines to a remote island in the South Pacific, a portable AED to a heart attack victim in the United States, or vital medical supplies to a wounded soldier on the battlefield, delivery drones have proved their worth. As drones become more sophisticated, there is no telling how they might impact medical care in the future.

SOURCE NOTES

Introduction: A Revolution in Delivery Service

1. Quoted in Jobinfo, "Domino's Just Made the First in the World Pizza Delivery by Drone," November 16, 2016. https://en.joinfo.com.
2. Quoted in BBC, "Amazon Drone Trial over Fleam Dyke 'Horrifying,'" August 1, 2016. www.bbc.com.
3. Quoted in B. Cameron Gain, "Drone Delivery Begins a Slow Takeoff," Transport Topics, January 13, 2020. www.ttnews.com.
4. Quoted in Sophia Rosenbaum, "Amazon Makes First Successful Delivery Using a Drone," *New York Post*, December 14, 2016. https://nypost.com.

Chapter 1: The Race to Be First in the United States

5. Quoted in Ian Bacon, "Virginia Town Becomes Home to First Drone Package Delivery Service," *Washington Post*, October 19, 2019. www.washingtonpost.com.
6. Quoted in David Pierce, "Drone Deliveries Are Coming: Jeff Bezos Promises Half-Hour Shipping with Amazon Prime Air," The Verge, December 1, 2013. www.theverge.com.
7. Quoted in Gain, "Drone Deliveries Begin a Slow Takeoff."

Chapter 2: Delivery Drones Around the World

8. Quoted in Transport Topics, "Drone Deliveries Become Reality as China Races to Take the Lead," July 3, 2018. www.ttnews.com.
9. Quoted in Bloomberg, "China Is on the Fast Track to Drone Deliveries," July 3, 2018. www.bloomberg.com.
10. Quoted in Jon Russell, "China's JD.com Tests Drone Delivery in Indonesia in First Overseas Pilot," TechCrunch, January 22, 2019. https://techcrunch.com.

11. Quoted in The Local, "French Postal Service Starts Drone Delivery in the Mountains," December 2, 2019. www.thelocal.fr.
12. Quoted in Christopher Mioms, "Your Drone-Delivered Coffee Is (Almost) Here," *Wall Street Journal*, March 30, 2019. www.wsj.com.
13. Quoted in Vidi Nene, "Aha! Drone Delivery Tested in Iceland," Drone Below, September 28, 2018. https://dronebelow.com.
14. Quoted in BBC, "Canada Moose Cree First Nation to Get Drone Deliveries," December 8, 2018. www.bbc.com.

Chapter 3: Designing the Perfect Drone

15. Quoted in John Porter, "Swiss Drone Crashes Near Children, Forcing Suspension of Delivery Program," The Verge, August 2, 2019. www.theverge.com.
16. Quoted in James Vincent, "Here's Amazon's New Transforming Prime Air Delivery Drone," The Verge, June 5, 2019. www.theverge.com.
17. Quoted in Megan Rose Dickey, "Uber Will Start Testing Eats Drone Delivery," TechCrunch, June 12, 2019. https://techcrunch.com.
18. Quoted in Nicole Kobie, "Droning On: The Challenges Facing Drone Delivery," Alphr, 2020. www.alphr.com.

Chapter 4: Delivering Health and Saving Lives

19. Quoted in Aryn Baker, "The American Drones Saving Lives in Rwanda," *Time*, 2020. https://time.com.
20. Quoted in *Time*, "Time 100 Next 2019," 2020. https://time.com.
21. Quoted in "Our Mission," Zipline. https://flyzipline.com/company.
22. Quoted in Baker, "The American Drones Saving Lives in Rwanda."
23. Quoted in "Ghana's New Lifesaving Drones: Like Uber but for Blood," Vox, June 4, 2019. www.vox.com.
24. Quoted in BBC, "Vanuatu Uses Drones to Deliver Vaccines to Remote Island," December 19, 2018. www.bbc.com.

25. Quoted in "Zipline, Which Delivers Lifesaving Medical Supplies by Drone, Now Valued at $1.2 Billion," CNBC Disruptor/50, May 17, 2019. www.cnbc.com.
26. Quoted in "WakeMed Health & Hospitals Joins Forces with UPS, FAA for Drone Pilot," Modern Healthcare, March 26, 2019. www.modernhealthcare.com.
27. Quoted in Future Stores, "How Flirtey Is Trailblazing Drone Delivery Services in the U.S.," 2020. https://futurestores.wbresearch.com.

FOR FURTHER RESEARCH

Books

Michael J. Boyle, *The Drone Age*. New York: Oxford University Press, 2020.

Alex Elliott, *Inside Drones*. New York: Rosen, 2019.

John L. Hakala, *How Drones Will Impact Society*. San Diego: ReferencePoint, 2018.

Kathryn Hulick, *How Robotics Is Changing the World*. San Diego: ReferencePoint, 2019.

Stuart A. Kallen, *What Is the Future of Drones?* San Diego: ReferencePoint, 2017.

Internet Sources

Evan Ackerman and Michael Koziol, "In the Air with Zipline's Medical Delivery Drones," *IEEE Spectrum*, April 30, 2019. https://spectrum.ieee.org.

Steven Ashley, "One of These Drones Could Save Your Life," NBC News, January 12, 2017. www.nbcnews.com.

Renee Knight, "Drones Deliver Healthcare," Inside Unmanned Systems, September 3, 2016. http://insideunmannedsystems.com.

James C. Rosser et al., "Surgical and Medical Applications of Drones: A Comprehensive Review," *Journal of the Society of Laparoendoscopic Surgeons*, July–September 2018. www.ncbi.nlm.nih.gov.

Tammy Waitt, "Self-Flying War Vehicle Coming to the USA," *American Security Today*, June 3, 2018. https://americansecuritytoday.com.

Websites

Center for the Study of the Drone (www.dronecenter.bard
.edu). A publication of Bard College, the website features a weekly
roundup of news about drones, including fixed wing, commercial,
and military drones. The website includes interviews with leaders
in the drone industry from government, business, and the arts.

DroneLife (www.dronelife.com). A blog with up-to-date news
and information about drone products, regulations, and business.
Includes a section devoted to drone videos and another to pod-
casts. Includes separate sections for specific industries, including
agriculture, mining, police and fire, delivery, real estate, surveying,
inspection, and construction.

Drones in Healthcare (www.dronesinhealthcare.com). A blog
that provides a roundup of the latest news in the medical application of drones. Includes exclusive interviews with medical drone
experts and links to relevant videos.

sUAS News (www.suasnews.com). Founded by drone pilots
and professions, sUAS News is the leading news and information
source for unmanned aviation. The website includes a searchable
drone safety map, color coded to indicate flying hazards such as
airports and ground hazards, as well as legal restrictions.

INDEX

Note: Boldface page numbers indicate illustrations.

The Advanced Drone Operations Toolkit (World Economic Forum), 27
aircraft, incidents of drones coming too close to, 42
Akufo-Addo, Nana, 48, **48**
Alibaba, 26
altitude, restrictions on, 13
Amazon, 17–18, 43
  cost of deliveries by, 7
  drone used by, 36
ambulance drones, 50
Army, US, 54
Association for Unmanned Vehicle Systems International, 15
Australia, drone deliveries in, 29
automated external defibrillators (AEDs), 53
autonomous, definition of, 14

Bezos, Jeff, 11–12, **12**
blood delivery, 44–45, 46–47, 48

Canada, drone deliveries in, 31–32
Center for the Study of the Drone, 59
certification, 15
China
  drone deliveries in, 5–6, 21–25
  use of drones in fighting Covid-19 spread, 31
commercial drone pilots, 15
communicable, definition of, 49
Covid-19 pandemic, use of drones in fighting, 31
critical-access hospital, definition of, 51
Cui Zheng, 24
CVS Pharmacy, **39**

Dada (website), 25
Defrance, Jean-Luc, 28
Delft University of Technology (Netherlands), 50
delivery chains, 7
delivery drones, **6, 23**
  accidents involving, 33–34
  costs savings from, 7, 24
  design/construction of, 38

PICTURE CREDITS